Y0-BRF-780

Haunted Places In York County Pennsylvania

By Leo Motter

To Minira,

Enjoy the ghosts!

Best wishes.

— Leo Motter

Copyright © 2005 by Leo Motter

All rights reserved. No part of this book may be reproduced in any form, except for the inclusion of brief quotations in review, without permission in writing from the author/publisher.

ISBN 1-59872-074-0

Published in the United States by Instantpublisher.com.

Additional copies of this book may be obtained by writing to the author at PO Box 3943, York PA 17402.

Table of Contents

Acknowledgements

I didn't make up any of these stories. I got them all from other people—either in print, internet, or first person accounts. Some of these people were there themselves and actually saw the ghosts, while others simply passed down a tale they had heard from someone else. I will admit taking some poetic license to help the stories flow better. But in their substance, they are intact.

I have tried to compile a list of most of the sources I used, for those readers who are serious students of York County's ghostly heritage. (See "Bibliography".) However, a few sources are so important that I need to thank them personally right on page 1.

First of all, the true masters of York County's ghosts are Georg R. Sheets and Fran Keller. Their ghost tour, held every Halloween in downtown York, is a huge amount of fun and I recommend it to everyone.

The library staff at the York County Historical Society also gave me invaluable help, digging out their thick file of "Ghost Stories" collected over the years. If you want to research haunted places in York, this is the first place you should go.

Kondor Media of Hellam produced a nice video called "Hauntings", which investigates several of York's ghostly sites. I'd like to thank Cher Kondor in particular for telling me the story of Codorus Furnace.

Thanks to the staff member at the Elmwood Mansion who showed me around the house and told me the stories. Thanks also for the leftover balloons you gave my son. You were very kind and welcoming.

To write the story of Camp Security's ghosts I needed to read the poem "Hessian Thal" by Henry L. Fisher. However, when I found it, it was written in Pennsylvania Dutch! Thanks to my favorite German scholars, Paul and Katie Weisser, who came to my rescue and translated it.

Special thanks to my three sons and fellow ghost hunters Michael, Luke, and Elijah, who accompanied me on most of my research trips around the county. These guys could face down the fiercest demon and laugh in its face.

Finally, none of this would have been possible without my wife, Tina Kent. Thanks Tina for all your help with editing, writing, driving, discussing ideas, and putting up with me. I will haunt you forever.

The Accomac Inn

Love, murder, hurricanes, war—from its wooded grounds overlooking the Susquehanna River, the Accomac Inn has seen all of these. Its history spans nearly 300 years, and includes many of the most important events in York County's past. If the stories are true, not all of that history is dead—some elements of it rest uneasily to this day.

The name "Accomac" is derived from the Nanticoke Indian word "Acaumauke", which means "across the water". The Nanticoke tribe was originally from Delaware and Maryland's Eastern shore, but fleeing the tide of European settlement they moved west to the Susquehanna River in the middle 1700's. Eventually they proceeded up the

River into New York and then Canada, but several remnants of their language were left behind.

"Across the water" is appropriate, because the Accomac Inn is located on land directly across the river from the town of Marietta. This section of river was used as a crossing point by settlers as early as 1725. A man named James Anderson received an official charter to operate "Anderson's ferry" on this section of river in 1742. Little is known of James Anderson, but there is some suggestion in the historical record that he may actually have been married to a native Nanticoke woman. It is clear that by 1775 "Anderson's Ferry Inn" existed on this site to provide food and shelter to the river travelers. The road running from the ferry to the town of Hellam was known as "Accomac Road" by 1750.

The first war to affect the Accomac Inn was the American Revolution. When British troops captured Philadelphia, the Continental Congress was forced to flee west to York, which served as the capital of the United States for nine months. Many officials of the revolutionary government crossed the river at Anderson's Ferry, and probably lodged at his Inn. The Marquis de Lafayette, for example, is known to have made that very trip on February 3, 1778. He wrote in a letter that the "river was full of ice", a sight many current residents would find familiar.

After the Revolution, the Inn and the ferry changed hands several times. A bridge was built across the Susquehanna River between Columbia and Wrightsville—the longest covered bridge in the world, stretching a mile and a quarter in length. This may have cut into the ferry's business a bit, but the Inn continued on.

In June 1863 the American Civil War came to York County when confederate troops captured the city. Refugees fled eastward to Lancaster County by both bridge and ferry, and suddenly the Susquehanna River became a military objective. If Confederate troops could capture a bridge across the river, they would be able to pour troops onto the eastern shore, setting them up to capture the city of Philadelphia.

One of the great mysteries of the Accomac is a gravestone by the side of the road, near the inn. A confederate soldier is buried here, but who he is or how he died is a matter of debate. Some say that he died from illness when stationed near the inn, and was buried by his comrades. Others say he was a spy who drowned while trying to cross the river. Although the truth will probably never be known, many spies were operating in this area, searching for a ford where Confederate troops might cross the river. One of them was shot in Marietta on June 28, 1863 after making the swim.

Military authorities believed that the Confederates would try to cross the Susquehanna at Harrisburg, so that they could capture a bridge and take the state capital at the same time. Consequently, most Union forces were concentrated in Harrisburg. Only a small group of about 175 volunteers were available to guard the covered bridge between Columbia and Wrightsville. The experts were proved wrong on Sunday, June 28, when the confederates sent a column of 2500 men to try to capture the Wrightsville bridge.

At 6 pm the shelling began. Anyone standing outside the Accomac Inn would have been able to hear the explosions and small arms fire echoing across the water. After about 90 minutes it became clear that the Union forces couldn't hold out against such overwhelming odds. They retreated back to the Columbia side of the river, and with night falling set fire to the bridge. The wooden planks caught fire quickly, consuming the world's longest covered bridge in a furious inferno.

Without doubt the sight from the Accomac must have been dramatic—a mile and a quarter of solid flame blazing into the sky, reflected in the waves of the river. Confederate forces never made it across the Susquehanna, and several days later they met defeat on the battlefields of Gettysburg.

The burning of the bridge was a tragedy for the town of Wrightsville, but it was a boon to the ferry operators, who now controlled the only means of crossing the river. The ferry at Accomac did well, and in 1864 it and the inn were purchased by a Mr. John Coyle. It was during the ownership of John Coyle that the most famous event in the Accomac's history occurred—one which continues to have ghostly echoes even today.

Around 1875, John Coyle gave the inn its current name of The Accomac. He and his wife Mary had a son named Johnny, who grew to be an expert riverman, knowing every cove up and down both shores. Despite his excellent boating skills, Johnny Coyle was generally acknowledged to be of "weak mind", probably borderline mentally retarded. There is also some indication that Johnny drank far too much of the inn's liquor. Between these two shortcomings Johnny made numerous mistakes in the ferry's ledgers, frequently angering his father.

In the early 1880's, John Coyle's wife Mary was becoming crippled with arthritis. She needed someone to assist her, so John hired a teenage girl named Emily Myers to come across from Marietta to live with them. Emily had been orphaned in Chambersburg at a young age, and she had no real home of her own. Reports from the time describe her as very beautiful, with dark brown hair and gray eyes. She liked to laugh and tease, and was a strong worker.

Young Johnny Coyle fell instantly in love with her. He couldn't get her out of his mind. Since they were living in the same house, it seemed natural to him that they should be married. Isn't that the way things like this worked? He proposed to her on numerous occasions, but apparently Emily did not find him quite so attractive. She turned him down again and again. Johnny couldn't understand it, and he grew increasingly frustrated.

On the morning of May 30, 1882, Johnny Coyle's desperation boiled over. He approached Emily as she was milking cows in the barn. He proposed to her one more time, and once again she refused. Johnny then pulled out a gun and pointed it at her, saying he would fire unless she agreed to marry him. Emily shook her head and turned away, replying "Johnny, I'm never going to marry any man."

Johnny pulled the trigger, shooting Emily in the chest. She died almost immediately.

Terrified at what he had done, Johnny Coyle fled into the wooded hills along the riverbank. Search parties were sent out, and after ten days he was captured and taken to prison in York. The population of York was infuriated at this apparently cold-blooded murder, so the judge shifted the trial to Gettysburg. The whole affair was front-page news for weeks. Finally on March 5, 1883 the jury found Johnny guilty of murder in the first degree. A round of final appeals was fruitless.

On the morning of April 22, 1884 Johnny Coyle had a final meal of Susquehanna River shad steak. He was then taken out into the jail yard, packed with over 300 spectators, and mounted the few steps to the scaffold. The sheriff placed a hood and noose over his head, and at 11:25 am the executioner pulled the lever that opened the trapdoor. Johnny's body twitched a few times as it hung. At 11:45 he was declared dead.

His mother Mary claimed his body, and transported it back to the shores of the Susquehanna for burial. His gravestone can still be seen there, just a short walk from the Inn.

But was that really the end of Johnny Coyle and Emily Myers? It was not long before mysterious things began to occur at the Inn. The barn where Emily had been murdered caught fire and burned to the ground. Shortly before midnight on May 16, 1935 a neighbor noticed that the Inn itself had caught fire. The proprietor and his wife were awakened from sleep and managed to rush out of the Inn with only the clothes on their backs. They watched while the whole building, full of valuable antique furniture, was completely destroyed.

Luckily the stone foundation remained, and the owner was able to reconstruct the Inn to look much as it had previously. Even in a new building, however, the spirits of the dead did not rest easily. Employees have reported feeling a strange presence in the Inn—a feeling of being watched, even in an empty room. Dishes have been moved from tables in the restaurant, and smashed on the floor. Doors have opened and closed all by themselves. One employee was walking through the Inn late at night when she began to hear music, and the voice of a woman.

There have even been sightings. A cook once saw a ghostly man sitting in the Inn's barroom. He did not seem at all threatening, and simply watched her for several minutes until she left. Occasionally a man's face has been reported looking out of an upstairs window—from a room that was known to be empty.

The ghost of Emily Myers has also been seen. A former employee once saw a young woman in strange, outdated clothing sitting on a step outside the Inn's back entrance. She had her head in her hands, and was crying. He tried to help her, but she waved him away. He had a feeling something was very wrong, and he telephoned the police. When they arrived, however, the woman had vanished.

On another occasion, a cleaning lady opened the door to an upstairs storage room, only to see the figures of a ghostly young man and woman standing in front of her.

More often, employees and visitors do not see actual figures in the Inn, but experience strange sensations. Some have reported catching a flash of something in a mirror as they walk by, or having a feeling of being watched. When they walk past certain doorways, employees have felt a surge of vertigo, as if the floor was suddenly moving beneath their feet. Whistling and music have been heard coming from empty rooms.

A local photo developer says that she received film from a local man several years ago. When she developed it, one picture showed the man and his wife smiling, standing in front of the Accomac Inn. And in between them stood a third figure—the ghostly form of a skeleton. The man was shocked—the skeleton hadn't been there when they took the photograph.

People in houses neighboring the Accomac Inn say that Johnny Coyle occasionally makes appearances at their homes too. Furniture is moved, and voices can be heard in various unoccupied rooms. It happened so frequently that one neighbor has been known to comment offhandedly, "Oh, that's just Johnny again."

So the next time you find yourself at the Accomac Inn, enjoying your grilled trout or your canard roti, remember two things: You're sitting only about 100 feet from the site of a ghastly murder. And someone may be watching you.

The Ghost Students of Lewisberry

When most people hear the term "Ghost Story" they expect to hear a tale about terrifying beings from the spirit world, who will threaten them and leave them shaking with fright. But if you listen to enough stories you begin to realize that not all ghosts are evil. Some appear lost or lonely. There are even those who are actively good, striving from beyond the grave to help those of us who are still alive.

The ghost students of Lewisberry fall into this last category—the good spirits, tragically killed at a young age, working to ensure that others don't suffer the same fate that they did.

They died at the intersection of Pleasant View and Wyndamere Roads, near the town of Lewisberry in northern York County. It is believed that they were football players, perhaps coming from a game at Red Land High School just up the road. It was night, and they were driving south on Pleasant View Road.

Even today this road is very rural, and when the sun goes down it becomes dark and forbidding. As you approach the intersection with Wyndamere, trees completely overhang the road, almost forming a tunnel. Walls of earth and vegetation rise up from the street, obscuring the driver's view. It is particularly difficult to see anything coming up Wyndamere Road from the south. This is a treacherous intersection, requiring a great deal of care.

High school students in those days were much the same as they are today, tending to underestimate danger and overestimate their own driving skills. You can almost picture them—a carload of guys, young and good looking, laughing loudly and not paying much attention to the road. Their headlights cut through the night.

When they reached the intersection of Pleasant View and Wyndamere they barely paused at the stop sign before gunning the engine. They shot out into the middle of the road. And this was their deadly mistake—they did not see the truck flying up Wyndamere Road, heading straight for them.

Brakes screamed but it was too late. The truck had no time to stop. It smashed into their car with an explosion of metal and shattering glass. The football players were killed instantly.

It was a terrible tragedy—young lives cut short. Now their obituaries are just yellowed bits of newspaper on a dusty library shelf. Their names have been lost to history.

But that is not the end of the story. You might ask this question: Is it possible to learn important lessons, even after you are dead? Some people say this is so, and that in death these young men have gained the wisdom they did not have when they were alive. They now know how dangerous this stretch of road really is.

Furthermore, there are those who believe that the young men have returned to haunt the intersection of Pleasant View and Wyndamere Roads. They are not there to frighten today's drivers, but to protect them. They want to prevent other teenagers from making the same stupid mistakes that they made.

If you go to this intersection you can experience their presence in a very real way. Drive south on Pleasant View Road until you come to the stop sign at Wyndamere Road. Your car will be facing downhill at this point. I would challenge you to put on your emergency brake and step out onto the road. Walk around the car and look at it carefully. From every angle, your car will truly appear to be facing downhill.

Now for the weird part. Get back in your car, and put it in neutral. Take off the brake. If the moon is right, and the spirits are with you, your car will actually *drift uphill!* Defying gravity, your car

18

will move backwards up Pleasant View Road. I guarantee this will freak you out.

Is this road a mistake of nature? How is it possible for your car to move against gravity? Some people believe that their cars are actually being *pushed* back uphill by the ghost students of Lewisberry. The spirits of these high school kids are there in the intersection, working to save unwary drivers from danger by pushing their cars backwards to safety.

A few observers have taken things a step further. They say that if you sprinkle baby powder on the front of your car while it is parked at the intersection, you will actually be able to see the fingerprints of the ghosts on your hood after it is pushed uphill.

Whatever the truth, this really is a dangerous intersection, so be careful. The last thing you want is to have an accident yourself. If you end up dead, you might have to spend all of eternity pushing other people's cars up the hill. And I would bet the young men's spirits won't be very welcoming to you. Even friendly ghosts aren't happy when humans ignore their warnings.

The Seven Gates of Hell

Something lies hidden in the rolling farmlands of Springettsbury Township. This is one of the most persistent legends of York County, passed down from teenager to teenager for nearly fifty years. Carloads of high school students have prowled this lonely country road, often dropping people off on a dare in the middle of the night to seek out "the gates of hell". Decades have passed, but the stories refuse to fade away.

Trout Run Road is in the northern part of the township. It remains peaceful and rural even today, although the nearby peach orchard is long gone. In the 1950's and 60's a large plot of land on the north side of this road was owned by an eccentric local physician, Dr. Harold Belknap. His property extended back beyond the Codorus Creek, and part of it was heavily wooded, impossible to see from outside.

Dr. Belknap did not like people coming onto his land. At one point he became so frustrated with trespassers that he put up a series of signs all along the north side of Trout Run Road. These signs bore the picture of a toad, and the warning "No Trespassing under the Sign of the Toad". (Dr. Belknap was apparently very fond of toads, and collected them.)

Because of these signs, people began to call this stretch of Trout Run "Toad Road". When these signs failed to deter interlopers, Dr. Belknap put up other more enigmatic signs at the entrance to his property, saying things such as "If you are found here at dusk you will be found here at dawn."

In front of the driveway to his house, Dr. Belknap erected a large and very ornate iron gate. It was readily visible from Trout Run Road, and well known to all the local residents. Beyond this gate is where the legend truly begins. Some locals say that the driveway off Trout Run Road ran deep onto Dr. Belknap's property, and was marked by a series of other gates. These interior gates could not be seen from the main road, and it would not be long before someone driving down that path would be deep in the dark woods.

These gates became known as "The Seven Gates of Hell", and were the subject of many whispered stories over the years. It was said that something was hidden at the end of this road, something which was not meant to be discovered.

People who proceeded down this road without permission were risking their lives—it was said that no one who had passed beyond the fifth gate ever returned.

What was it that could have been hidden on Dr. Belknap's property? Another local rumor says that there was a building far back in the hills, known as "Dr. Belknap's Fresh Air Sanitarium". A sanitarium was a place where people often went 50 or 100 years ago to recover from illnesses. These could be physical illnesses, such as tuberculosis, or mental illnesses such as depression or schizophrenia. Sanitariums were frequently located in natural settings such as mountains or woodlands, where it was thought the clean air and pure waters could promote healing.

Some say that Dr. Belknap's sanitarium was dedicated to treating the criminally insane. Notorious stalkers, murderers and molesters were locked up here far back in the hills, where the latest psychological techniques could be safely applied to them.

The goal was to cure them, but these men and women were the worst of the worst. Some of them were beyond insane—they could only be described as evil. On a few occasions, it is said that a nightmare came true—several of the criminals escaped. They hid in the rugged countryside, and would kidnap or murder anyone they encountered. Some of these criminals were never recaptured, and may still be wandering deep in the hills to this day.

Locals who knew Dr. Belknap say these legends are nonsense. They insist that he was a heart expert, and that he had no interest in treating psychiatric patients, much less the criminally insane. They say there never was a sanitarium, and that there were no gates beyond the initial one. Is it all just a story (perhaps promoted by Dr. Belknap with a wink to keep away trespassers)? Or could there be some truth to the 50 year old legend, that there is something still stalking the dark woods, waiting for the next victim to wander innocently by?

Codorus Furnace

Everyone has a secret, something they have tried to bury and forget. Sometimes those secrets are so powerful that they refuse to go away, even when the people guarding them are long dead. Is this why the figure of a woman in white has been seen walking at night on the hill behind Codorus Furnace? Could some terrible, secret crime have been committed here, years ago?

Codorus Furnace doesn't look like the scene of a crime. It is a tranquil site, located near the spot where the Codorus Creek empties into the Susquehanna. The road here is quiet, with few cars. Standing on the old stone foundation, the only sounds you can hear are the creek rushing by below you, and the occasional rustle of an animal in the underbrush. On the weekends, you might see kayakers paddling down the waterway, or hikers walking the nearby trails.

The furnace itself seems almost like a fading memory—as if the forest might swallow it up again if it was left alone for a few years. Already the old house on the hill above it has been invaded by small trees and bushes, and is slowly crumbling back into the earth.

But it was not always this way. Two centuries ago this was a site of bustling industry, filled with billowing smoke and the clang of steel on steel. The furnace was originally constructed in 1765 by a man named William Bennet. Iron used to be a big business in York County, with upwards of 170 iron mines in the County in the 1800's. The Dillsburg region probably produced the best iron, but the ore for Codorus Furnace came mainly from the nearby Hellam hills and from Chestnut Ridge in Lancaster County.

The original owners of the furnace unfortunately got into debt, and ended up selling it to James Smith, a local lawyer who was a signer of the Declaration of Independence. Smith owned the iron works throughout the Revolutionary War, and used it to produce cannonballs and other armaments for the rebel army. The ironworkers were very patriotic men, strong supporters of independence.

Despite its importance to the American war effort, Codorus Furnace was not very good for James Smith's wallet. Over an eight year period the furnace lost $25,000, and Smith ended up selling it as well. It continued to operate into the mid-1800's, processing local ore into iron for sale at the furnace itself and in the markets of the surrounding townships.

One of the last furnace masters was a man named Trego, who lived in the nearby furnace house. Trego ran a tight ship, and was strict with his workers. When it came time to give out their pay, the forge workers would line up at the kitchen window, where Trego's wife handed them their money. If one of the workers became drunk or violent, Trego would throw them down in the basement of the house, where he had a room with bars on the doors.

Some people have speculated that other things may have gone on down in this basement—unspeakable, evil crimes that were later covered up. No details are known, but speculation was raised after a human skull was found hidden under the floorboards. Why was it there? What good reason could there be for a family to hide a skull under its floor? I have a tough time thinking of one.

The skull itself might be explained away, if it were not for the ghost. The white figure of a woman has been seen exiting the main house, and walking down the hill toward the forge. Her identity is a mystery. Was she one of the former residents of the house? Or could she be a nameless victim, of a forgotten crime?

This is the dark secret of Codorus Furnace, and we will probably never know the truth. But it is a secret that refuses to lie buried. The forest slowly grows, year by year erasing all signs of human habitation on this piece of ground. And the woman's spirit continues to walk, searching for a justice she will probably never find.

Freeborn Garrettson

One of the most familiar characters along
the roads of the early United States was the
Methodist circuit preacher. Given the great size of
this new nation there weren't enough ministers to
serve each community, so the Methodist Church
came up with the idea of having clergy who
traveled instead of serving at only a single church.
One preacher would ride a "circuit", preaching at
many small churches and gatherings along the way.
Some of these circuits were small, including only
four or five churches, but others spanned hundreds
of miles over rough dirt roads. Along the lonely
roads, these holy men sometimes encountered not
just good, but also deadly evil.

The circuit preachers were usually hardy young men, most in their twenties and thirties, who struck out on a horse with nothing but a Bible and a hymnal in their saddlebags. They rode through rain and snow, preaching nearly every day, and enduring great physical hardships. One preacher noted that he regularly was forced to swim through creeks and swamps, and spent entire days wet from head to foot. They endured hunger and illnesses, and half of them died before age 33. There was no corner of the country where they could not be found, and no weather they would not brave, leading to the famous phrase "There's nothing out today but crows and Methodist preachers."

One of the best known circuit riders was named Freeborn Garrettson. He was born in Maryland in the year 1752, and converted to Methodism at age 23. After his conversion he freed his slaves and began a traveling career which was to span more than 50 years. He preached at churches from Canada to North Carolina, and brought thousands of people into the faith. When he died at age 76, he was the oldest circuit rider in the Methodist Church.

Freeborn Garrettson's journeys brought him even to the wilds of western York County. In his autobiography, he describes an eerie encounter that occurred somewhere in the farmlands off the East Berlin Road in 1781. In those days this was a dark and desolate area, with long distances between farmhouses. He was trying to make it to the town of East Berlin, but it was nighttime and he took a wrong turn. Soon he was hopelessly lost in the cold darkness.

As he was passing a farmhouse he heard the sounds of moaning and weeping coming from inside. Clearly, someone here was very upset about something. Being a man of God, he pulled up his horse, and got down to see if he could be of assistance. He knocked at the door. It was answered by a woman.

One glance told him that she was the one who had been crying. The expression on her face was a mix of terror and agony. But seeing he was a preacher, she was able to calm down and invite him in. She was alone in the house.

"I thought you might be Satan," she told him. "I've been waiting for him."

This was an interesting turn of conversation. Reverend Garrettson asked why she might be expecting a visit from Satan.

"I've done something unforgivable," she replied, her voice cracking again. "I sold my three children to the devil. He'll be coming soon to claim them." With this she broke down into full-blown sobbing again.

Was she mad? Freeborn Garrettson had traveled extensively, and seen much. He had encountered many people her age, both men and women, who had lost their minds. Such people could live for years in lonely farmhouses, undiscovered by outsiders. Or, on the other hand, could she have had a true encounter with the Prince of Darkness? He had also known things like that to happen, on his journeys.

"He won't get my children, though," the woman went on. "I've hidden the children at a neighbor's farm. I won't let him take them." Despite the tears, there was a hardness in her eyes.

Freeborn Garrettson told the woman that she did not need to be afraid. "Satan has been conquered by the blood of the Lamb, which is Jesus. The evil one cannot harm you if you dwell in Christ." He spoke to her at length, quoting scripture, outlining the hope she would have if she gave her life over to Jesus.

The woman listened to what he said, but she seemed skeptical. "He is coming," she insisted. "I know he is coming."

"Even if he did come," Garrettson continued. "He can't take your children. You could not have sold your children's souls to Satan. Their souls do not belong to you. Your children belong to God, and the devil has no dominion over them."

The woman shook her head, unconvinced.

"Please believe me, your children are safe," Garrettson said. He invited her to come to the service he was planning to celebrate the following day in East Berlin. There she would hear more about the power and love of God, and of God's ability to command demons. He insisted over and over that she come to the meeting, and finally he wore her down—she agreed to attend.

It was deep in the night when Garrettson stood to depart. When he walked across the yard to his horse he encountered a man, standing in the doorway of the barn. It was the woman's husband. He shook Garrettson's hand.

"Thank God you came," the man said. He explained that his wife had been speaking about the devil for weeks. The husband himself had sent the children off to their neighbor's farm, for the children's protection. "She keeps a razor in her dress," he explained. "She says she'll kill the children herself before she lets the devil steal them away."

Garrettson nodded his head, and mounted his horse. Soon the farm disappeared behind him in the blackness.

The following day at the revival, Garrettson scanned the crowd. True to her word, the woman showed up. Garrettson read the scriptures and preached on them, directing much of what he said straight at her. He watched as her doubting expression softened, and she warmed to his words. By the end she came up to him and said she was experiencing "a wonderful calm."

Garrettson stayed just a few days, and then, as circuit riders do, he rode on to the next town. He would never meet the woman again, but he was convinced that by the time he left she had become "a blessed, pious woman", and that her children were safe. No demon and no evil deed would visit them there on the road to East Berlin.

Peggy LaRue

This is what got her killed—she was leading a double life. In the first life she was a respectable wife and mother of two. She worked as a nurse in Patterson, New Jersey, and her name was Alice May Abbott. But when she decided to run off with a local justice of the peace, she began her second life. She showed up in Central Pennsylvania in a new flapper dress and a bobbed haircut. The world of hospitals and patients was left behind. She moved now in a flashier world of parties, jewelry and bootleg whiskey. She changed her name to Carmen "Peggy" Larue, a glamorous name to fit her exciting new lifestyle

It was 1924, an era of Prohibition, gangsters, and high living. But the golden glow of the party life did not last long. The justice of the peace soon left her, and Peggy Larue fell in with a seedier crowd. She found herself living in a whorehouse within view of the Susquehanna River in Columbia, Pennsylvania. She had developed a taste for illegal alcohol, and she sometimes came across to York County to find it.

On August 9 she was at the Crystal Restaurant on North George Street in York with her date, David Dorwart of Lancaster. They met up with two friends, Lenora O'Bryan and Fred "Sailor Kid Mack" McLean. McLean was AWOL from the U.S. Navy, and claimed to have been a boxing champion in the Hawaiian Islands. The group made their way to Toot's speakeasy, located in a lumber yard in south York, where they began some serious drinking.

Once they were good and drunk the group decided to go for a drive in the countryside outside York City. They drove up Carlisle Road to the area north of what is now Bannister Street. At the time this was still rural farmland, popular among the locals as a makeout spot. Not much making out got done this night, however. Peggy Larue had drunk a quart of whiskey and was very sick. Fred McLean, also roaring drunk, passed out in the car.

Lenora O'Bryan decided to take advantage of the situation, and robbed the unconscious McLean. She grabbed about $180 in cash from him as well as his .32 revolver.

When McLean came around he realized that his money and his gun were gone. He began to shout with intoxicated fury, then attacked O'Bryan and wrestled the gun back from her. He turned the

34

gun and shot her in the face, shattering her cheek but not killing her. McLean then shot at David Dorwart who had started running across the fields. The bullet struck Dorwart in the hand, but he managed to escape. Finally McLean turned to Peggy Larue, lying drunk in the road. He pointed the gun at her and shot her in the head, killing her.

McLean was taken into custody by York Police. He was found guilty and sentenced to 20 years in prison. The York Dispatch wrote of his trial, "McLean is sorry he killed Peggy Larue. He is also sorry he shot Dorwart. But he does not regret wounding Lenora O'Bryan."

Was justice done here? Twenty years is not a long sentence for murder, particularly since Peggy Larue was innocent of any crime against McLean. If the woman McLean had shot had been the respectable Alice May Abbott, nurse and mother, he may well have received life in prison, or the death penalty. But the life of Peggy Larue, prostitute and drunk, apparently was considered by the courts to be less valuable.

Whatever the reason, the spirit of Peggy Larue does not seem to have rested easily in the years since her murder. Already in early 1925 locals reported hearing mysterious screams and moans coming from the area around the murder scene. These were so common that people began to speed up their cars when they passed, or avoid the place entirely.

A local farmer gave the most detailed account. He said that he was driving past the area around midnight, in the dead of winter, when he saw a woman dressed in white standing by the side of the road. According to a story in the York newspapers, he said "I wondered what a woman in night clothes, as she appeared to be, could be doing out at that late hour exposing herself to the cold." When he approached he saw that she was wearing a white cap and uniform "like trained nurses wear". Her eyes appeared to be very sad.

The farmer stopped his car and offered her a ride. But as he drew nearer to her she backed up into a snow bank and vanished.

This area of Dover Road and Bannister Street has now been developed into the suburbs surrounding West York High School. But does the ghost of Peggy Larue still wander these streets, on late winter nights? If so, it appears from the farmer's story that the image of the flapper and party girl has been washed away, leaving behind only the melancholy nurse, her true identity. In death there is no more deception.

The Cookes House

Ever since it was constructed the Cookes House has been known for its hospitality. During Revolutionary War times it served as a tavern, where some of America's founding fathers dined and slept. During the nineteenth century its cozy rooms hid runaway slaves. And today, the house plays host to visitors of a different sort. Mysterious, ghostly lodgers have apparently decided to move in, and have made it known that they aren't planning to leave anytime soon.

The Cookes House seems out of place—a picturesque limestone mansion that looks like it was transported forward in time 250 years and dropped in the middle of a residential neighborhood. Johannes Guckes constructed it in 1761 on land that has now become the city's Martin Luther King Park. For a while it was considered the finest home in York west of the Codorus Creek. Back then the house would have been surrounded by trees and farmland, away from the bustle of downtown York.

It was a quiet inn, in a quiet city. In the mid 1700s York was a slow place on the frontier where nothing much ever happened. Then the American Revolution erupted, Philadelphia was overrun by British troops, and York suddenly found itself the temporary capital of the United States.

Waves of refugees and famous men poured across the Susquehanna River, fleeing the fires of battle. It didn't take long for all the hotel rooms in this little city to be snatched up by members of the Continental Congress and their staffs. Hotel rooms in the downtown area near the square were highly prized, and hard to get. Late-coming patriots and hangers-on found themselves shut out, and they were forced to look for lodgings in private homes, or in the countryside.

Even such a stellar figure as Thomas Paine, author of the famous revolutionary pamphlet "Common Sense", was unable to land a room in downtown York. He was one of the many who eventually was welcomed into the Cookes House, where he spent quite a bit of time during the nine months Congress met in York.

After the Revolution, York went back to being a quiet market town. But other historical forces began to sweep through the area. The Industrial Revolution brought train lines and factories to the region. And the growing tensions between the free north and slave-holding south became very evident in York County, with a large stretch of the Mason-Dixon Line along its lower border. The Underground Railroad brought a stream of runaway slaves up from Maryland, across the Pennsylvania border into York, and then on north to Canada. Local tradition holds that the Cookes House played a role in this great endeavor, hiding fugitive slaves from time to time within its walls.

In the twentieth century the city of York began to grow quickly, and residential housing construction spread into the outlying farmland. Before long the Cookes House was completely surrounded by neat grids of streets packed with homes. The tavern business faded away, and the Cookes House itself fell into decay. On several occasions the house narrowly avoided being demolished. Luckily in the 1970s a few historically minded people decided to restore it, and it is now listed in the National Register of Historical Places.

Even today however the Cookes House is not a museum—it remains a private home, owned and lived in by regular residents of York. And those residents have reported some strange happenings over the years. The ghost of a blonde girl wearing a dress has been seen playing in one of the upstairs bedrooms. Her identity is a mystery. Could she have been the young daughter of Johannes Guckes and his wife? Was she a tenant in years past? Could she have died in the house? No one knows.

Footprints have been found in the dirt floor of the basement in the morning after it was swept. Someone has been heard walking around the house at night, when it was known to have been empty. Is this the young girl, or are there other spirits present in the house?

The ghost (or ghosts) appear to be active. On one occasion a mattress was thrown across a room. On another, a tree stump was thrown through one of the windows. Sometimes a cold presence is felt in the rooms, and a few visitors have been gripped by an unexplained feeling of fear.

Are the spirits angry? Or are they simply trying to protect the house from unknown intruders? Residents themselves have never felt threatened. On the contrary, they report feeling a strong sense of inner peace in the house. Perhaps the ghosts are just making themselves at home, trying to be good guests, like all the others before them who have been welcomed into the Cookes House.

Cannibal

This is a story about how treachery thousands of miles away and 150 years in the past can continue to haunt us today. It begins about as far from York County as it is possible to get—in the Fiji Islands, in the South Pacific Ocean.

In the middle of the nineteenth century, American whaling ships were making frequent contact with the natives of Fiji. The Chief of the island of Bau was a cruel man, addicted to alcohol. For a few crates of whiskey he would occasionally trade an entire island to the whalers, which greatly upset the people who lived on those islands. Unfortunately he was also the most powerful warrior in the archipelago, and had conquered almost every occupied rock in his part of the ocean.

Only the warriors of the island of Lovani held out against him. After years of battle, it became clear that he would never be able to overcome them by military means alone. He would have to resort to trickery. On one of the island holidays, he invited the warriors of Lovani to a peaceful celebration. After they showed up, he got them drunk on kava fruit. When the warriors woke up, they found that they had been sold into captivity—not as slaves, but as employees of the Barnum and Bailey Circus.

In the nineteenth and early twentieth centuries, the Barnum and Bailey Circus was one of the biggest attractions in the entire United States. Its trains would pull up in rural communities and set up huge tents full of acrobats, elephants, lions, and other exotic sights. In an age before movie theaters and television, the circus was often the most exciting thing the farmers and small town merchants saw for weeks. They would pour out of their shops and barns and spend fistfuls of hard-earned dollars to see the latest wonders.

Agents of the circus visited every corner of the earth, searching for ever newer freaks and esoterica to fill the sideshows. One such agent was traveling with the whaling ships when they happened upon the captured Lovani warriors. Immediately he came up with the idea for a new show—Cannibals! He would dress them up in native clothing and jewelry, and parade them before the Midwestern farmers as fearsome south-seas cannibals. The warriors from Fiji became one of the Circus's most popular attractions.

Thus it was that one day in the late 1800's a train car full of so-called cannibals from Fiji pulled into the city of York. They were housed in the old Penn Hotel, which was located across the street from the Strand-Capitol Theater downtown. From there they were transported to the circus tents, to perform their fearsome Polynesian dances and rituals before the people of York.

Unfortunately, having lived all their lives on isolated islands in the middle of the ocean, these Fiji natives were not accustomed to the common diseases of the cold and rainy United States. A germ that caused only mild symptoms in a native Pennsylvanian might affect these men very differently, causing severe illness. They frequently fell ill, and had to be excused from their performances.

This is what happened to one of the Fiji warriors on the night they arrived in York. When he arrived at the circus tent he told the others that he didn't feel well, and he returned to the hotel room. The others did their performance and returned to the hotel late at night, only to find that their comrade had been sicker than they thought—in fact, he had died right there in the room.

What happened next is a matter of controversy. One newspaper report says that officials from the circus later arrived in the room, to find that the Fiji warriors were in the process of eating their newly deceased friend! Another newspaper denies this report, and says that they were simply getting him ready for burial.

Whatever the truth was, it is certainly true that the funeral for the Fiji man was one of the biggest events of the day. Having no money and no affiliation with any church in the area, he was buried in the local Potter's field across from Penn Park. (Today this site has become the parking lot for Saint Patrick's Catholic Church.)

A big funeral procession was held, and the warrior was dressed in his traditional Polynesian garb. He had rings in his nose and ears, as well as on his fingers. Bracelets were on his arms and native weapons were in the coffin with him. Reporters from local newspapers attended, along with a huge crowd of spectators. He was laid to rest in his grave, and a few days later the Barnum and Bailey train pulled out of town for good.

For years, the Fiji warrior was the most famous occupant of the Potter's Field cemetery. People knew exactly where his grave site was, and visited it often. Decades passed, and everything was peaceful until it came time to build the new York High School downtown. Architects decided that the best site would be the Potter's Field cemetery, and so the graves would all have to be moved to a new cemetery in north York.

When it came time to dig up the coffin of the old Fiji native, a crowd gathered around the site. They had all heard the stories of his exotic dress and his tattoos, and wanted to see it for themselves. The shovels of the workmen broke the dirt, and the hole took its rectangular shape and grew deeper.. Finally they scraped against wood. The crowd held its breath as the coffin was lifted out of the grave, and the lid was opened.

But this is where the mystery of the Fiji warrior began, because when the coffin was opened there was nothing in it. It was completely empty. No skeleton, no bracelets, no exotic spears. Just an empty wooden box and a big pile of dirt. How could this be, when the funeral had been so public and so well-attended?

The rumors began soon after that. People reported sightings of a small, dark-skinned man in strange clothing wandering the streets of downtown York, late at night. Could it be that the warrior from Fiji somehow escaped from the grave, and continues to wander the streets of York today? Could he be searching for a way to return to his far-off island home? Or does he want revenge against the men who enslaved him, and placed him in a freak show on the opposite side of the earth?

We will probably never know what actually happened to him, but it's probably a good idea to be safe. So if you're on the streets of York late at night and happen to run into a strange man with tattoos, a nose ring, and a big spear, make sure you are very, very polite.

The Imp of Clark Alley

Of all the spirits that haunt York County, the Imp of Clark Alley may be the most bizarre. Most people think of ghosts as grey or translucent human beings, walking or floating above the ground. Even an invisible ghost, speaking or moving objects around a room, wouldn't be all that unusual. But when was the last time you heard of a ghost appearing as a vase, or a barrel of beer? Yet that is exactly the sort of thing the Imp has been said to do.

Clark Alley (now known as "Clark Avenue") is located right in downtown York, between Philadelphia and Market Streets. It runs a long course through town for many blocks, usually past the back entrances of houses and restaurants. But occasionally there are flashes of beauty, such as a colorful mural or a bed of flowers.

No one knows where the Imp of Clark Alley came from—there is no story to explain it. It seems to be a classic poltergeist, a rogue spirit interested more in mischief than in any serious horror. In January of 1880 the number of sightings exploded, and the York newspapers contained numerous accounts of it. So many people reported seeing the Imp that a kind of game developed. Parties of half-drunk men would set out at night through the streets of downtown, trying to find (or better yet, catch) the Imp.

The area of Clark Alley between Beaver and George Streets appears to have been the Imp's favorite haunting spot. Occasionally it would appear there in the form of a man, pretending to be a horse thief. Another time it came as a paperboy, but when searchers approached, he suddenly vanished "in a cloud of smoke". Where the paperboy had been standing, the searchers found a piece of paper. On it were written words "in foreign and unmeaning characters". The scrap of paper smelled strongly of sulfur.

The Imp's strangest habit was appearing in the form of inanimate objects. It was said to have appeared once as a demijohn—a large glass bottle or vase surrounded by wicker. Another time the Imp attacked a party of searchers by taking the form of a barrel of beer, tapped at both ends. It rolled down the alley toward them, causing them to scatter in different directions into the darkness.

On one occasion, a party of searchers encountered the Imp as a patch of swirling, formless darkness. One of them drew his gun and fired at it, causing it to vanish. When they went to investigate, they found a wooden post with the bullet embedded in it.

The final reported sighting of the Imp was on January 30, 1880. A woman was sweeping the sidewalk in front of her house in the early morning hours, when suddenly she saw a tall woman dressed all in black walking slowly down the opposite side of the street. Realizing it was actually the Imp, she became terrified and ran into her house, slamming the gate. Several other people reported seeing the same figure on the street before it vanished.

Since that dark month more than a century ago, not much has been heard from the Imp of Clark Alley. This would be in keeping with the typical behavior of a poltergeist, which tends to pick one area to haunt for a while, and then moves on to cause mischief somewhere else. Then again, we can never be sure. Clark Alley seems peaceful today, but you shouldn't completely relax. On a dark night, walking up the avenue with your friends, take care when you hear a rumbling on the street behind you. It could be a ghostly beer barrel, headed in your direction.

Maybe the Imp lives on.

Revolutionary Ghosts

If you're the sort of person who likes to tour graveyards, two that you definitely can't miss are Prospect Hill Cemetery and the churchyard of First Presbyterian Church in York. Not only are both of them historic and picturesque, but both of them are haunted—and by signers of the Declaration of Independence, no less. James Smith was a lawyer and resident of York, while Philip Livingston was from the state of New York and just happened to be visiting here when he died. Both were great patriots, although their personalities could not have been more different.

The period from September 1777 to June 1778 was probably York's greatest moment in the national spotlight. British troops had captured

Philadelphia, and the Continental Congress was forced to flee west across the Susquehanna River. For nine months, York served as the capital of the newly formed United States of America. Many important documents were written here, including the Articles of Confederation—the forerunner of the U.S. Constitution. Legendary figures such as James Madison, Thomas Paine, and the Marquis de Lafayette could be seen walking on Market and George Streets. They stayed in local homes and ate in local taverns.

In those days York was the wild west—a small border town populated mainly by German immigrants. To outsiders, it could seem almost like a different country. John Adams wrote, "Multitudes are born, grow up, and die without ever learning the English." The Continental Congressmen, used to the niceties of Philadelphia society, were not very impressed by this rough frontier town. "This York Town is a vile quarter," one wrote. "The (dirt) streets and its Dutch inhabitants are happily assimilated."

Despite the fact that they were looked down on by their leaders, the people of York responded vigorously to the call of revolution. One diarist of the time wrote, "York Town seems quite deserted on account of the departure of all men under fifty years of age. Our young men had to leave for the army in Jersey."

James Smith was one of the most avid supporters of independence. He was born in Ireland, but had immigrated to America as a boy and attended the University of Pennsylvania. For a while he was the only lawyer in York. He was an energetic and very social man, fond of a good joke and a glass of wine.

Some other energetic and social men in Boston ended up propelling Smith onto the national scene. After the Boston Tea Party, the British government passed the so-called "Intolerable Acts", dissolving the elected Massachusetts Assembly. Smith was outraged. He organized the first company of volunteer soldiers in Pennsylvania with the aim of resisting the British, and marched them to New Jersey.

Smith also became a politician, serving as a member of the Continental Congress from 1776 to 1778. When the Declaration of Independence was presented on July 4, he signed it without hesitation. In the eyes of England this made him a criminal with a death sentence on his head. When Philadelphia was attacked he fled with the rest of the Congress back to his home town of York. Here he continued his work of shaping the new nation.

Philip Livingston, on the other hand, was anything but vigorous. At age 62 he was one of the oldest members of the Continental Congress—and he wasn't a healthy 62 either. Livingston was sick with "dropsy", a state of swelling in the limbs and abdomen that we would today attribute to chronic liver disease or congestive heart failure. He felt that he was dying even before he came to York, to the point where he said his final farewells to his family before leaving. Despite this premonition of doom, he pulled himself up, determined to do his duty as a member of Congress, and rode on horseback all the way here.

Having arrived in York, Livingston took up a room in a hotel and rarely left it. He spent the last month of his life in great pain, apparently suffering from an abdominal ailment. Gouverneur Morris visited him, and wrote, "This I gather from a quick pulse, languor, continued sickness, some pain and much uneasiness about the part I supposed to be affected (his stomach) a decline of strength and flesh, hectic appearance." He finally died on June 12, 1778.

Livingston's funeral was a major event in York, just as a funeral for a member of Congress would be today. All the members of the Continental Congress were present, and every man wore a black armband. There was a procession to his burial spot in the churchyard of the German Reformed Church (originally located on Market Street near where the Woolworth Building stands today).

Even in death, however, Livingston could not rest in peace. The new Prospect Hill Cemetery was opened in 1849, and Livingston's body was moved there along with all the others in the German Reformed cemetery. Eventually his grandson, Stephen van Rensselaer, sponsored a large monument on the site.

James Smith survived the Revolution and went on to lead a successful career as a lawyer in York. He was elected to the Pennsylvania State House of Representatives in 1780, and in time was promoted to Brigadier General of the State Militia.

He finally died on July 11, 1806, and was buried in the cemetery of First Presbyterian Church.

The ghosts of both Philip Livingston and James Smith have been reported on a number of occasions. James Smith is said to appear as vivacious in death as he did in life, laughing or raising a drink. Livingston, on the other hand, appears bloated and morose. He looks like a man who never wanted to come to York in the first place, and who lived his last month here in misery. I like to think that Smith may be trying to cheer him up, showing him that if you have to be stuck haunting someplace for all eternity, this "vile quarter" isn't such a bad place to do it.

William Goodridge

The story of William Goodridge is a story of how great good can be accomplished even in the most evil times. His house still stands on North Philadelphia street, as a monument to his heroic actions before and during the Civil War. Even though Goodridge himself was forced to flee this house, other presences appear to have been left behind. These presences can still be heard and felt today, although whether they are true ghosts or simply a residue of the painful times in which Goodridge lived, we will probably never know.

Goodridge's rise from humble beginnings is almost worthy of a Hollywood screenplay. He was born a slave in Baltimore in 1805, the son of a white man (presumably his owner) and a black mother.

At the age of six he moved to York. Since Pennsylvania was a northern state, it is assumed that this is the point at which he gained his freedom. He became an apprentice in a tanning factory owned by Reverend William Dunn.

The details of his early life are sketchy. At the age of sixteen he left the tannery and traveled around the Northeast. When he returned to York two years later, he had married a woman from Maryland named Emily. He opened a barbershop downtown and quickly became successful. At the time, it was perfectly acceptable for a black man to work as a barber—many of the barbers in York, in fact, were black.

Goodridge invested his earnings from the barbershop in other businesses. Soon he opened his own confectionary store, selling such things as candy and jewelry. Using his experience as a tanning apprentice he bought and sold animal hides. As his wealth increased he bought a number of buildings in downtown York. He even went on to construct the five-storey Centre Hall, which for a while was the tallest building in York.

His boldest business move was investing in the new railroad industry, and it paid off for him handsomely. He established the Goodridge Reliance Line, consisting of thirteen railroad cars serving a number of communities around eastern Pennsylvania. This railroad line made him even wealthier. It is estimated that his personal worth was between $50,000 and $200,000—a fortune for the middle of the nineteenth century.

In the space of a few decades, Goodridge had risen from slavery to become one of the most successful businessmen in the city of York. He was well respected, and had a wonderful family as well. His three sons, Glenalvan, Wallace, and William, opened one of the first photography studios in town in 1849, and became quite well known. From the outside, Goodridge appeared to be a model of the American dream, happy and content.

But beneath this surface, Goodridge was living another life—a secret life. Despite his successes he could never forget his earlier years as a slave. The very thought of slavery sickened him. He vowed to fight it in any way that he could. At great risk to his businesses and even his life, he became involved in the fugitive slave movement known as the underground railroad.

Goodridge had several advantages in this struggle. First of all, he lived in the city of York, which was located only fifteen miles from the border of Maryland—a slave state. Escaped blacks who made it over the border would have a fairly short journey to reach his protection. Second of all, Goodridge owned buildings in which to hide the refugees, and he also had a way of transporting them further north to safety. Third and perhaps most importantly, he was a wealthy and respected citizen, whom few would suspect of being involved in such a dangerous and illegal activity.

To hide runaway slaves, Goodridge constructed secret panels on the third floor of his Centre Hall building. He could move people into and out of this building under cover of night, and they could remain hidden from his customers throughout the day. He also built hiding places in his own home, at 123 East Philadelphia Street. There was a trench located beneath one of the buildings behind his house, lined with straw. In addition, there was a secret trapdoor in his kitchen, which opened onto a staircase leading down into a dark basement chamber. Runaway slaves could be kept in both of these places. Located safely in his own house and his own place of business, it was easy for Goodridge to feed and care for these people until they had regained their strength.

Unfortunately, even though the slaves had made it north of the Mason Dixon line, they were not yet free. The United States Congress had passed the Fugitive Slave Act, which stated that any runaway slaves who were caught in the north had to be returned to their owners in the south. True freedom was only possible if they made it all the way north to Canada. Many slavecatchers prowled the streets of border towns like York, hoping to cash in on reward money offered by the wealthy plantation men. It was not safe for fugitives to remain in York for long—once they were ready, they would have to move on, or risk recapture.

Goodridge had an excellent means for moving the runaway slaves—his railroad cars, which departed York on a regular schedule for points east. Hidden among bags of grain and produce, they could be safely transported to other havens of the Underground Railroad across the river in Columbia, or further east as far as Philadelphia.

It is impossible to know how many people Goodridge was able to move along his railway from slavery to freedom, but estimates range into the hundreds. Slaves were not the only fugitives he hid, either. Goodridge was also involved with the radical abolitionist movement, which vowed to oppose slavery by any means possible—even violence. After John Brown's raid on Harper's Ferry, Virginia in 1859, several of the conspirators were forced to flee. It is said that Goodridge hid one of these men, Osborn Perry Anderson, in the secret rooms on the third floor of Centre Hall. He remained there for several weeks, and then was moved to Philadelphia on Goodridge's railway line. Eventually Anderson made it all the way to Canada, likely following the same route as the runaway slaves.

Goodridge continued his work through the early years of the Civil War. But his career was brought to an abrupt end in 1863 when General Robert E. Lee decided to invade the north. The city of York was occupied by confederate forces in June 1863, and Goodridge was forced to flee with his family to Minnesota. From there he saw his ultimate dream fulfilled—the defeat of the south in the Civil War, and the end of slavery forever. But he never returned to York, and he died in Minneapolis in 1873.

Goodridge's house still stands today, marked by a historical plaque, on a pleasant stretch of North Philadelphia Street. As with Goodridge himself, however, the peaceful appearance may hide a dark secret. Some people have heard voices coming from the secret room in the basement where runaway slaves were hidden. Others report hearing babies screaming, or women crying. The flight out of bondage was long and arduous, and not all of the runaways survived. It is said that some of their ghosts may linger in the cellar of the William Goodridge House. Although it was a place of safety, this house still stands as a reminder of the great pain millions of black Americans had to endure in the name of racial inequality.

The Spirits of Penn Park

If you believe that ghosts tend to haunt places that were sites of death and suffering, then York's Penn Park should be packed with ghosts. Sure, it looks peaceful enough now—the sort of place you might go to run your dog or play with your kids. But don't be fooled. This grassy ground has had plenty of blood spilled on it, from accidents, amputations, and executions.

Originally called Penn Common, this land was used since the founding of York as a public gathering place. The descendants of William Penn gave it to the city under the condition that it remain "a public common forever". It was made into a public park in 1890, but prior to that it had a variety of functions.

During the Civil War, for example, Penn Common was converted into a military hospital. Someone walking by in 1862 would have seen the grass crisscrossed by long rows of cots, which were filled with wounded soldiers brought North from the fighting. Night and day, the cries of the wounded echoed through the streets. People of the town came forward to nurse and feed them. Food, water, and medical supplies were donated to the hospital by local businesses. Despite the best efforts of the people of York, many soldiers died, and many more had to endure lost limbs and painful surgeries. Even when they survived their wounds, the soldiers faced the threat of diseases such as cholera and dysentery.

The hospital reached a crisis point when General Lee's forces invaded the North in June 1863. As Confederate forces under General Gordon approached York, they announced that they planned to burn all government buildings in the city, including the hospital. All of the patients in the hospital had to undergo emergency evacuation across the river to the town of Columbia. Those who were in good enough shape to walk were organized into companies to defend the bridge at Wrightsville. The seriously ill were moved into a hastily erected facility at a school.

Luckily, the Confederate occupation of York lasted only a few days. The troops marched west to join the Battle of Gettysburg, leaving so quickly that they never had a chance to burn the city down. Not only was the hospital at Penn Park reopened in the following days, but it became busier than ever.

Hundreds of wounded soldiers from Gettysburg were brought there for treatment. The hospital continued to operate through the remainder of the war, treating an estimated 14,000 soldiers by the time the war ended in 1865.

The main ghosts reported at Penn Park, don't date from the Civil War period however, but from an earlier conflict—the American Revolution. It was May 1781, and General "Mad Anthony" Wayne was quartered in York with his troops. He had just come from fighting in New Jersey, and his troops were tired and demoralized. The war had been going on for five long years, and the number of men in his force was badly diminished. General Wayne made a number of public speeches in York, in an attempt to recruit a few volunteers. But finding new men willing to fight was tough at this point in the war, and General Wayne was having trouble just holding onto the soldiers he already had. The men were restless, and some even talked of deserting or rebelling.

Money was a big problem for American soldiers. When the Continental Congress declared independence from England, they stopped using British money and began to print their own American currency. This is what the troops were supposed to use to buy supplies and rations from the towns they encountered. However, the value of the currency had dropped dramatically over the course of the war, to the point where it was now barely worth the paper it was printed on.

When General Wayne's troops tried to pay for equipment using American currency, some of the shopkeepers in downtown York refused to accept it. They told the soldiers that they would only take silver or gold, or the reliable old British money. Furthermore, some of them even tried to agitate the troops, telling them that they should refuse to follow orders until they were paid in currency that was actually worth something.

This made General Wayne's men even angrier—not only were they tired and hungry, far from their homes, but they didn't even have the means to purchase the supplies they needed. They were preparing to move out of town, marching south to join General Lafayette's troops in Virginia. There were rumors that a big battle was coming— one that could decide the war once and for all. Who could say if any of them would survive it?

Under these circumstances, a few men snapped. As the troops were forming up to leave York, a number of them (some sources say three, others say seven) refused to leave until they were given their pay in hard currency. Other men sympathized, although they continued to follow orders for the time being. Everyone watched to see what General Wayne would do. His judgment came down firmly—the men were to be publicly executed for disobeying orders.

How should a commander react in this sort of situation? It was wartime, he had no hard currency to give his men even if he had wanted to, and he needed to move out quickly to fight a major battle. Some have criticized General Wayne's actions as unnecessarily harsh. But any sign of weakness might have led other members of his force to conclude that it was okay to refuse orders. The planned march out of York might have fallen apart, the ranks paralyzed by lack of discipline. Without Wayne's men to reinforce Lafayette at Yorktown, it is possible the climactic battle of the American Revolution could have gone differently.

The doomed men were brought to Penn Common and stood up before a firing squad. General Wayne later wrote about this event: "Whether by design or accident, the particular friends and messmates of the culprits were their executioners. And while the tears rolled down their cheeks in showers, they silently and faithfully obeyed their orders without a moment's hesitation."

The rifles fired, and the rebellious men were blown apart. Newspaper reports carry gristly reports of blood and brains being spattered across the ground. "Even devils shrank back and stood appalled", one witness wrote. The mangled bodies were gathered up by their fellow soldiers. It is likely they were buried across the street in the local potter's field (now the parking lot of St. Patrick's Church).

General Wayne achieved his objective—he had no further trouble with rebellion. The troops marched out of York without incident. They linked up with General Lafayette, and in October 1781 they participated in the final defeat of British troops at the battle of Yorktown. The war was over, and America was finally free.

But the spirits of the rebellious soldiers did not rest peacefully. Over the years, many people have reported seeing mysterious figures wandering the silent hills of Penn Park at night. Some say they are dressed in revolutionary war uniforms. Others report that the men bear grotesque wounds, including missing limbs and even a missing head.

Is this part of their eternal punishment, to wander Penn Park forever? A romantic might imagine that they are still striving to carry out their duties as American soldiers, guarding the city and the nation from its enemies. Or could it be that they are searching for revenge, perhaps against the selfish merchants of eighteenth century York, who convinced them to rebel in the first place?

We may never know. But one thing is for sure—this is probably the most blood-soaked patch of ground in York County. No one should be surprised to find something eerie wandering here under the trees after the sun goes down.

The Elmwood Mansion

If you are trying to find the most haunted house in York, look no further than the Elmwood Mansion. No other home has such a variety of spirits seen by so many people over such a long span of time.

The mansion itself was constructed in 1835 by a prominent local businessman named Jacob Brillinger. Brillinger had started off as a simple farmer and livestock manager. As his business boomed, he constructed other industries on his property including a creamery and a distillery. He became quite wealthy, and decided to build an extravagant home where he would live after his upcoming marriage.

The home was three stories tall, built of brick with white pillars in the Greek Revival style. Overlooking the main road, its wide porches and balconies would have provided a magnificent welcome for summer party guests. The rooms inside are large and airy, filled with natural light from a multitude of windows.

Unfortunately Brillinger was not as lucky at love as he was at farming, and his planned marriage fell through. Brillinger decided to immerse himself in business and politics, and took on the position of director of the York Bank. In the years leading up to the Civil War he was a passionate supporter of the Union. Local tradition holds that he was involved with the Underground Railroad, hiding escaped slaves in the attic of his mansion and in the cellar of the old farmhouse. A trapdoor in this attic leads to a back staircase, which was thought to be an escape route for slaves. It is said that signals were sent to Underground Railroad activists in other parts of the city using lights in the attic windows. In 1863, with the Civil War raging, Brillinger enlisted as a humble private in an independent company of Union soldiers.

The Civil War seems to have left its mark on the Elmwood mansion, since most of the mansion's ghosts appear to date from that period. After the War ended, the house was sold to the Small family, who lived in it for three generations. It is the Smalls who first began to report supernatural activity.

There are at least two spirits who have been encountered in the mansion. The most common one is a young girl dressed in a Civil War-era hoop skirt, who has been seen descending the main staircase and exiting the front door on multiple occasions. Her identity is unknown, although people who work in the mansion have nicknamed her "Virginia".

Virginia's appearance can be disturbing. In some cases only the lower half of her body is seen coming down the stairs—a skirt and feet, with no head or torso. Some say that when she appears the lights in the house flicker, and animals appear very agitated. Other witnesses report hearing her skirts rustling in silent rooms, and cleaning staff have found the footprints of a woman in the plush carpet of one of the rooms after it had been cleaned.

A former owner says that she has heard music coming from one of the upstairs rooms, as if a young person were practicing for a recital. After doing some research, the owner found out that that room had indeed been used as a music room by one of the earlier occupants. Over the years several psychics have visited the Elmwood Mansion, and they have reported feeling a sense of tension between Virginia and her father.

The other figure reported by the Small family is called "The Gray Man", seen gazing out of an upstairs window. He has one hand on his hip and the other hand on the hilt of his sword. Most people believe that this is the ghost of a Confederate soldier from the Civil War. He may have occupied the Elmwood Mansion in the short period of time rebel troops controlled the city of York in 1863, before the Battle of Gettysburg. He is said to have a melancholy appearance, but has never shown any sign of anger or violence toward any of the mansion's occupants.

Is it possible that this man was killed at Gettysburg, along with so many of his fellow southerners? If so, perhaps he returns to the Elmwood Mansion because it was the last place he felt a sense of peace, before the great clash of armies. The wide porches and grand scale of the mansion may have reminded him of his home in the Old South. Or perhaps he comes here to taunt the descendants of his enemy, Jacob Brillinger, who was away fighting for the Union army while Confederate troops occupied his house.

Details of the lives of both Virginia and the Gray Man have been lost to history, but some people have constructed a fanciful story around what is known. They speculate that perhaps Virginia was the daughter of the Confederate soldier, and that the tension felt in the house comes from the fact that she and her father were fighting over one of her romances.

Perhaps she was in love with a Union soldier, and her father appears tense at the window because he knows the relationship is doomed. A mural painted on the back staircase of the mansion depicts this story, with Virginia and her blue-coated suitor in the foreground, and her angry gray-coated father standing back near the mansion watching them with his hands on his hips.

Other strange presences have been felt in the mansion as well. One former owner saw the nearly invisible ghost of a cat down in the basement. He also reports hearing the ticking of a clock coming from a room in the house where no clock was present. Doors and windows have been found opened in the house when previously they have been locked. Security staff have found lights on in the building after it had been closed down. On other occasions, motion detectors in the mansion have been tripped when no one was inside.

The Elmwood Mansion continues to be used today, not as a residence but as a place for holding conferences and parties. Long tables and internet hookups have replaced much of the grand old furniture. But despite these modern additions, the ghosts here do not seem to have faded away with time. People still occasionally sleep in the upstairs bedrooms, and some who work and visit there continue to report ghostly encounters.

Given the number of encounters, the wide variety of people who have had them, and the continuing reports of sightings, I think we can say this with confidence—if you're one of those strange people who actually wants to encounter a ghost, the Elmwood Mansion is probably the place to go.

Camp Security

Most of York County's ghosts appear to be friendly, or at least neutral toward the human beings they encounter. The ones seen at Camp Security, however, are different. People who have seen them describe them as full of fury, seeking revenge against those who left them trapped on this lonely piece of ground so many years ago. Let's just say they aren't the sort of guys you'd want to run into accidentally on a dark night.

Camp Security was a prisoner of war camp during the American Revolution, located at the southern end of what is now Springettsbury Township. Today the site of the camp itself has been lost, ploughed under cornfields and covered by trees. One section of the camp has been turned into

71

a playground, with benches and swingsets, and children laughing in the sunlight. But just take a short walk up the path beside the creek, and you'll soon begin to see what things were like in this area in the 1700's. As you climb over decaying trees and hear the invisible animals rushing away through the bushes, you may begin to pick up some of the uncomfortable, eerie feeling that hangs around this place.

The camp has its beginnings in the Battle of Saratoga, which took place in New York State in September and October of 1777. In the first phase of this battle, British forces attacked the ragtag Americans and "won", but in the process lost two men for every one the Americans lost. In the second phase of the battle, four British soldiers died for every American, and the Americans scored a major victory. Some people consider this the turning point of the Revolution—once the countries of Europe saw that the Americans were capable of winning battles, support for the new nation began to pour in. The French joined the war on the American side, contributing greatly to our victory.

After the British forces surrendered, the Americans were left with several thousand prisoners of war. The Continental Congress marched these prisoners through the winter snow up to Boston and then down to Virginia before finally instructing the army to construct a prisoner of war camp for them in York. Central Pennsylvania was considered safe American territory, far from any British troops who might try to free the prisoners. Construction on the camp was begun in August 1781, and soon between 1000 and 2000 prisoners were housed there.

The prison itself was on about 20 acres of land. Chestnut trees were cut down and sharpened at the top end, then used to build a 15 foot high fence around the main stockade. Inside this stockade, stones were collected from the fields and used to construct huts for the prisoners to live in. Many of the British prisoners actually had wives and families here in America, who followed them down to York after their capture. These families built their own huts on the land surrounding the main prisoner stockade. Camp Security became a small city, home to thousands of men, women, children, and prison guards.

As prisoner of war camps go, Camp Security was one of the more lenient. The relationship between the British prisoners and their American guards was very good. After a few months, most of the prisoners were allowed to leave the main stockade, and go to live in the outside huts with their families. Many of them set up little businesses making lace, belt buckles, pins and other trinkets. If they behaved well, they even got passes to go into the city of York to sell these items. The patriotism of the young men of York had sent them to fight in Washington's army, and there was a shortage of labor on local farms. British prisoners were willing to help out, serving with area farmers as indentured servants.

Most of the British prisoners came to enjoy life at Camp Security, and they had no desire at all to escape. When a new prisoner named Sergeant

Roger Lamb tried to organize a prison break in 1782, he could find almost no one in the camp who wanted to join him. In disgust, he later wrote "I perceived that they had lost the animation which ought to possess the breast of the soldier."

This is not to say that everything in the camp went smoothly all the time. There was a dark side to Camp Security. A gallows stood in a prominent place in the camp, constructed by cropping the branches on two trees and placing a crosspiece between them. It wasn't just there for decoration.

One occasion on which the gallows was used was when a group of prisoners abused their liberty. A party of British soldiers were out in the York countryside on passes, when they began to knock angrily on the door of a farmhouse. The farmer, who was named William Morgan, recognized who they were, and refused to let them in. This made the prisoners even angrier. They pulled out weapons and fired a few shots through the door, injuring Morgan.

A neighbor rode his horse to the camp, and raised the alarm. The camp guards took an immediate roll call of the prisoners, and marked down who was missing. When they returned, the men were placed in special detention. Eventually they were put on trial, and sentenced to be hung. This was done at the hanging tree, in view of all the other prisoners. Although the gallows is no longer present today, it could be seen rising up above the cornfields until well into the nineteenth century.

The greatest tragedy to hit the camp occurred in the winter of 1782-83. An epidemic fever (some say smallpox) swept through the prisoners and their families, leaving many of them dead. In an attempt to cut the spread of the disease, the dead were buried quickly, in shallow graves marked with rough-hewn stones. According to a statement from a former resident, these graves were still visible early in the twentieth century, "on the west side of the creek, on the crest of the hill near the woods". At some point, however, the graves were robbed by local physicians, who were in search of skeletons for their studies. Some of these skeletons may still be around today, in downtown doctors' offices or in dusty attic crates.

Disease and grave robbery—is this the reason the spirits of Camp Security appear to be so angry whenever they show up? The graveyard seems to be the site where sightings have been reported most often. The most famous account of these ghosts was written by a nineteenth century York lawyer, Mr. Henry L. Fisher, in his poem "Hessian Thal". In it he describes how the ghosts appear at midnight every Christmas Night in the area of the former graveyard.

"Then go with me on Christmas Night/Out there into the Hessian Valley/Then you will hear the lonely cry…" The ghostly soldiers call out the names of their officers, and then scream "It is your fault/That we are imprisoned in Hessian Valley/So far from our homes and friends!"

Will the ghosts of Camp Security ever rest peacefully? Perhaps they might, if their bones were collected and re-buried, and the gravesites were treated with respect. We should probably acknowledge that this is a historical military cemetery, one of the few places were foreign soldiers are buried on American soil. Until that happens, however, I wouldn't recommend trying to find these ghosts, especially around midnight. These are a few spirits who probably wouldn't be too happy to see you.

Margaretta Furnace

In the mid-1800's, the fires of Henry Slaymaker's iron forge lit up the small town of Margaretta Furnace with a hellish orange glow. Iron ore melts at 3000 degrees, and once the furnace is hot the fires would never be allowed to go out. Night and day the forges were stoked with charcoal, producing a continuous blaze that would last for months at a time. Molten iron was poured into molds, and hammers rang out across the farmland as sweating men pounded it into shape. Although the ironworkers have faded into history, there are reports that the ghost of the forge's owner, Henry Slaymaker, may still haunt this quiet valley.

Margaretta Furnace began as a small cluster of buildings that grew up around the furnace. These included workmen's houses, a grist mill and cider mill, a general merchandise store and confectionary. Henry Slaymaker oversaw all of the town's operations from his stone mansion. He dominated this area so completely that he became an almost legendary figure.

Between the Revolutionary War and the Civil War, the countryside of Pennsylvania was dotted with small iron forges like Margaretta Furnace. Many of them were located near streams, so that the flowing waters could power the bellows that kept the fires hot. An abundance of trees could be cut down and used as fuel. Iron ore and limestone went into the forge, and out came pots and pans, axes and hammers, stoves and anvils— many of the necessities of early American life.

Henry Slaymaker made a bit of money from the forge, and in addition to his mansion was able to build two large stone barns—a mule barn, and a hay barn. The first barn alone was said to be large enough to house 100 mules. These were located between Ore Washer Run and the Canadochly Creek. Just above the hay barn, in the side of a hill was the opening to a small, dark cave.

Margaretta furnace operated from 1823 to 1854. Around the middle of the nineteenth century, small charcoal-fired forges were replaced by coal-powered factories, and then by huge industrial steel plants like those owned by Andrew Carnegie in Pittsburgh. The town of Margaretta Furnace lived on after the forge itself was closed, and from the stories the locals tell it seems that something else may have lived on too in the area of Slaymaker's old property.

In the late 1800's, about a dozen young men from Margaretta Furnace returned from fighting the Civil War and decided to found a group called "the Honery and Secret Order of Helbenightians". It appears that this order existed for two main reasons: #1 Drinking, and #2 "Raising Hell" at night (hence their name). To join the group, a man had to pay an "initiation fee" of one jug of hard cider. Upon the death of any member, the dead man's family had to pay the "death benefits", which consisted of enough hard cider to get the rest of the members roaring drunk.

The Helbenightians met in an abandoned house, which was reported to be full of ghosts. Spoonie Gohn, a man who certainly put away his share of hard cider over the years, was a leader of the group. On several occasions, Spoonie claimed to have seen the ghost of old Henry Slaymaker come out of the cave near the hay barn, carrying a lantern blazing with a flame a foot wide.

One night Spoonie was walking home from a night of drinking, carrying a hunk of cheese he planned to eat for his breakfast. He dropped his cheese and was searching for it, but apparently it was too dark and he was too drunk to find it, so he lay down to sleep. He was aroused several hours later by the ghost of Henry Slaymaker, which was scratching the bottom of his foot. Spoonie ran home, terrified. When he returned the next day he found his hunk of cheese lying by the side of the road, but no signs of the ghost.

In yet another encounter, Spoonie claimed that he was attacked by Slaymaker's ghost as he was walking home. Spoonie said that he threw the ghost into a ditch, then leaped on top of it. He held the ghost down while he got out his pocketknife. He then proceeded to stab the trapped spirit multiple times, until its guts spilled out over the dirt.

The following day, on their way to work, the other Helbenightians walked by the area in the hope of seeing the disemboweled ghost. They found no dead body and no blood, but they did find the impression of Spoonie's corduroy pants in the ditch, as well as multiple stab marks in the mud from Spoonie's knife.

Spoonie Gohn and the other Helbenightians are long gone now, but Margaretta Furnace continues on as a quiet modern community. More recently one of the residents of the town claims to have seen a mysterious carriage drawn by two horses emerge from the area of Slaymaker's old barns and come down the driveway. Before it reached the main road, the carriage vanished.

Henry Slaymaker's ghost may still haunt the area around Margaretta Furnace. If you're in the mood to investigate these sightings, the Helbenightians give the most likely way to succeed. First, drink a great quantity of hard cider. Second, go for a walk down a dark path along Ore Washer Run or the Canadochly Creek late at night. Don't forget to bring along your knife, since this spirit has been known to attack. And be very careful never to drop your cheese.

The Ghost of the
Immaculate Heart

    If you want to avoid being haunted by a
dead friend or relative, follow one simple rule:
Don't make them any promises you don't intend to
keep. Nothing seems to irritate ghosts more than a
broken promise. A case in point is the ghost that
haunts Immaculate Heart of Mary Church, in
Paradise Township.

    The land where Immaculate Heart of Mary
now stands was once owned by a devout Catholic
couple named Frederick and Magdelena Brandt. In
the early 1800's they bought over 200 acres in this
area, and prospered with their farming and mill
business. Since at that time Catholic churches were

81

rare in this part of the county, they used part of their house as a mass chapel.

Despite their faith and their wealth, the couple died childless. Having no heirs, they wished to use their money to help other children in the community. They willed their property to the Jesuit order of Catholic priests, with the stipulation that there be "established thereon as soon as convenient a school or seminary or any other house of education for the purpose of bringing up youth in useful literature and Christian piety."

The Jesuits accepted the gift gratefully, and they kept using the house as a chapel for many years. Eventually a church dedicated to the Immaculate Heart of Mary was constructed in the 1840's on the property. The Catholic community of Paradise continues to benefit from the Brandts' generosity to this day. However, the Jesuits neglected to found any sort of school on the property, and it did not take long for mysterious troubles to begin.

The priests began to hear strange noises around the house at all hours of the day and night. Doors opened and closed as if by some invisible hand. At night while the priests slept, sheets and covers were torn away from their bodies. It was clear that something strange was going on.

There was a large cupboard in one corner of a room where the priests used to store their ceremonial vestments. Several times they came into the room to find the vestments scattered across the floor. The cabinet doors themselves would open and close, and noises seemed to be coming from inside. On at least one occasion, there is even a report of an old lady jumping out of the cupboard to frighten someone in the room!

Many people came to believe that the house was being haunted by the ghost of Magdelena Brandt, who was angry that her wishes for a religious school on the land were being ignored. Some people in the parish began to grow nervous about worshipping in a building that was occupied by an unhappy spirit. The pastor at this time was Father Steinbacher. He decided he would attempt to solve the ghost problem through prayer and fasting. He prayed to God that the spirit haunting this place be confined to the cupboard where the vestments were stored. After he made this prayer, he moved the cupboard down into the basement where it wouldn't bother anyone.

This seemed to do the trick. There were still occasional reports of noises coming from inside the cupboard, but the rest of the house was peaceful. In the years that followed, the house changed hands several times, and there are reports that people would come from as far away as Baltimore to visit and spend a night in the haunted house.

One of the house's owners, Mrs. Agnes Wagaman, attributed the mysterious sounds in the cupboard to a rat's nest she once found there, and she blamed the sounds in the rest of the house on a treebranch which rapped against one of the walls. But there are other people who aren't so sure.

Immaculate Heart of Mary continues to be a thriving parish, ministering to the people of western York County. Its setting could not be more peaceful—surrounded by tall trees and acres of rolling farmland. There are few outward signs that any ghosts remain there.

The famous cupboard may be a different story. It has been fully restored, and is on view to the public every other Sunday at the John Timon Reily Historical Society in McSherrystown. Could any traces of Magdelena Brandt's spirit remain there? Certainly no one has reported seeing any elderly ladies leap out of it any time recently. But until her wishes are fulfilled, I'm not sure I would want to spend a night alone in the same room with it.

The Train Jumper

Young people feel that they're immortal. How else can you explain the array of crazy stunts all of us used to pull when we were younger? Most of the time it's just innocent fun—a quick thrill, a laugh, and it's over. But once in a while the stunts turn deadly.

Such was the case with 10 year old Hiram Hall. In 1886, one of the more popular games among kids in York County was hopping trains. In those days the trains were pulled by big black steam engines, trailing clouds of black coal smoke for miles. These were the foundation of the new industrial economy, the fastest way to travel up and down the eastern seaboard, or from coast to coast. They hauled crates of merchandise, or cars full of passengers through the rolling Pennsylvania farmland. For kids in the small villages around York County, the arrival of a new train would be one of the most exciting events of the day.

Train hopping worked this way—as a train rattled through your town you could run alongside of it, jump up and grab hold of a railing or a ladder. If you held on long enough, and escaped detection by the railroaders, you could ride the train all the way into York or Baltimore. The champion of all train jumpers, Bob Kuntz, could hop a train going 30 miles per hour. At that speed, as soon as he grabbed the railing he would be slammed against the side of the train. But he held on, and rode into legend.

The rail line from York to Baltimore in the 1880's ran through the sleepy community of Seven Valleys. It was there that young Hiram Hall made his run. He leaped up to catch a ladder on a box car. But his hand missed the rungs, and he fell onto the rails. The train ran over him, severing both legs at the knees.

The townspeople of Seven Valleys rushed to help him, but his injuries were too severe. He lived only four hours. A contemporary account in the York Daily Record says that by the end he was "begging townspeople to kill him because of the pain". His death most likely came from shock, after major blood loss.

Today the train line has been converted into a "Rail Trail" park. On sunny days, friendly retirees walk along it smiling and waving, while young people tear past on mountain bikes at killer speed. You're not likely to encounter anything more frightening than a hawk or a stray turtle.

But when the sun goes down, the trail takes an eerie turn. Some people have reported encountering the spirit of a young boy along the trail at night, between Seven Valleys and York. The spirit does not seem malevolent—more lost, or frightened. He bears the marks of a terrible accident, and some even say he asks them if they have seen his lost legs.

Perhaps the young Hiram Hall is still dazed and wandering more than a century after his accident. He may be confused, still trying to figure out what happened on that tragic day so long ago. But perhaps he is here as a warning today's children—that life is fragile, the days of summer are not endless, and that death can come for the strongest of us at a moment's notice.

Hessian Prisoners in Hanover

Everyone knows the first part of this story: General George Washington on Christmas night, 1776 crosses the Delaware River with his army of ragtag American revolutionaries and launches an attack on British forces camped in Trenton, New Jersey. Most of the enemy troops based here are mercenaries hired by King George III to reinforce his own forces in the American colonies. These foreigners are nicknamed "Hessians", because most of them come from the Hesse-Cassel region of Germany.

Because of a raging snow and hail storm the Hessians do not send out their usual patrols, and they are completely surprised by Washington's attack. After only 90 minutes of fighting the

Americans score a crushing victory, with only four men wounded in battle and two frozen to death in the snowstorm. The Hessians, on the other hand, suffer 106 men killed or wounded, and 868 are captured. It is the first great American victory of the Revolutionary War, and is celebrated up and down the thirteen colonies.

All of us learned that much in grade school. But what about the next part? What ever happened to the 800 Hessian troops captured in the Battle of Trenton? Does anyone care? Well, if you are a ghost hunter in York County you should care. Not only did the Hessians pass through York, but if the legends are true some of them may still be here.

From Trenton the Hessian prisoners were shipped westward into Pennsylvania, away from the front. The Americans wanted to keep them as far from British forces as possible, to avoid attempts at rescue and cut down on attempts at escape. The ultimate destination would be the new prisoner of war camp in Frederick, Maryland, known today as "The Hessian Barracks". But this camp was not constructed until 1777, and the winter weather made many of the rough dirt roads impassable. The trip to western Maryland from New Jersey would have taken many weeks at best.

Along the way, the prisoners passed through York County, and in particular through the small town of Hanover. Today Hanover is a major manufacturing area, one of the fastest growing parts of the county. But in 1777 it was very rural, with only a handful of buildings and a Lutheran and a

Reformed church rising up out of miles of rolling countryside.

No one knows how many cart loads of prisoners passed through Hanover on the way to Frederick. But it is said that the old Hanover Pike (known today as Route 194) is haunted by their spirits. An old story in the *Hanover Record* reports that a man and woman in the 1800's were riding their horses up this road when they took shelter in a covered bridge, at the point where this road crosses the Conewago Creek.

Their horses became very restless and refused to move any further. The two people squinted in the dark bridge, trying to see what was frightening their horses. Suddenly in front of them they saw two larger horses approaching them, pulling a large sleigh. In the sleigh were a dozen men "of almost gigantic stature". They were dressed in uniform, and appeared to be military officers. The sleigh passed by in total silence, coming so close that the woman could have stretched out her hand and touched it. The ghostly soldiers gave no sign that they saw the couple, and as soon as the sleigh emerged from the bridge it vanished.

Most people who hear this story believe that the military men were some of the prisoners of war from the Battle of Trenton, on their way to Frederick. The fact that they were in a sleigh implies that they were being transported in the winter. At the time of the Revolutionary War there was no covered bridge over the Conewago—it was only a ford, or shallow crossing point in the creek.

Why would spirits choose to haunt this spot? Is it possible that some tragedy occurred here? Perhaps the creek was swollen from melting snows, to the point where it swamped the sleigh and drowned the bound prisoners. Did their dying screams echo unheard across the dark farmlands, all those years ago?

We will never know. The covered bridge is gone now, but other sightings of the soldiers have been reported along this road over the years. After the war, many of the prisoners at the Hessian Barracks decided to stay and settle in Maryland and Pennsylvania. They felt quite at home among the German-speaking farmers and merchants here. Their descendants are among us today, working beside us in office buildings and factories. And maybe some of their forefathers are still with us too, guarding a lonely stretch of road outside Hanover.

Powwow

Powwow is central Pennsylvania's own homegrown form of folk magic. It is impossible to understand the story of Rehmeyer's Hollow without some knowledge of powwow. In the Pennsylvania Dutch tradition, there are two basic sorts of magic: *Powwow*, which is "white magic" directed toward healing the diseases of humans and animals; and *Hexerei,* a form of "black magic" directed toward casting curses and summoning supernatural creatures to do one's bidding. A century ago, belief in these two forms of magic was so strong and all-pervasive in York County that people could be driven to commit murder in order to break a hex.

The roots of powwow extend all the way back to superstitions of the Dark Ages, which were carried across the ocean by German immigrants. In the eighteenth and nineteenth centuries, medical science was not very advanced. When the farm people of York became sick, they were just as likely to present themselves to a powwow practitioner (or "braucher") for healing as they were to see a medical doctor. Powwow was not seen as a secretive set of rituals, performed in the dark by superstitious crackpots. The more skilled brauchers were well known and respected members of York County society. They advertised in the newspaper, went to church, and often were able to make a good living. Their numbers have diminished significantly in recent years, but a few continue to practice in remote farm communities even today.

For the most part, the rituals of powwow were passed down orally from one generation to the next. Fortunately, some of these practices were written down and collected into books. The best known of these is "The Long Lost Friend", written by John George Hohman and published near Reading, Pennsylvania, in 1820. This book was circulated widely in the nineteenth century and became extremely influential. Faithful followers of the powwow art believed that simply owning a copy of the book would provide protection against evil influences. "Whoever carries this book with him," Hohman wrote, "is safe from all his enemies, visible and invisible."

One fundamental fact that is clear from reading Hohman's book is that powwow practitioners did not believe that they were performing cures themselves. True healing power came from God—the powwower was only a vessel through which God's healing would flow. At the beginning of his book Hohman quotes the forty-ninth Psalm: "Call upon me in the day of thy trouble, and I will deliver thee, and thou shalt glorify me."

Many powwow rituals employed verses lifted directly from the Bible. For example, it was believed that bleeding could be stopped by quoting Ezekiel chapter 16 verse 6: "Then I passed by and saw you weltering in your blood. I said to you, live! Yes, I said to you when you were in your blood, live!"

Other formulas invoked the name of Jesus, Mary, or one of the saints. For example, it was possible to use a divining rod to find underground water by holding the wand in your hand and saying "Archangel Gabriel, I conjure thee in the name of God, the Almighty, to tell me, is there any water here? Tell me!" Another tells that pain can be stopped and wounds healed by waving a wand and saying, "With this switch and Christ's dear blood, I banish your pain and do you good!"

Other charms covered a whole range of topics—everything from healing warts ("Roast chicken feet and rub the warts with them, then bury them under the eaves") to curing tuberculosis, to protecting your horse from worms. One favorite tactic was for the powwower to write a "himmelsbrief" or magical letter full of prayers and invocations of the Trinity. A person could carry this letter in a pocket, or sleep with it at night, where it would provide healing and protection. A particularly complicated himmelsbrief or one written for a particularly severe condition could cost the patient quite a bit of money.

It wasn't enough for a braucher to simply speak the correct words and perform the correct motions. To be an effective powwow doctor, a person had to have "the power". (Some people have suggested that the word "powwow" comes from the German pronunciation of the word "power", rather than from the Native American festival.) This power of healing could be inborn, or it could be passed from one person to another.

Traditionally, it was believed that "power" could be passed only to a member of the opposite sex—for example, from a mother to her son, or a father to his daughter, but not from mother to daughter or father to son. There were exceptions to this rule, but certainly the practice of powwow was not restricted to one gender. Women, who were often barred from practicing medicine or other formal professions, were able to attain quite prominent positions as brauchers.

Both men and women who practiced powwow were called "witches" by their neighbors in Central Pennsylvania. (The masculine term "warlock" was never used here.) A "witch" was not necessarily a woman, and witches were not necessarily seen as evil. Those who practiced the healing arts, such as Hohman taught in "The Long Lost Friend", were viewed by their neighbors as good and acceptable members of society.

It was a different story, however, for those who practiced hexerei, the dark side of

Pennsylvania Dutch magic. Men and women who did powwow for their neighbors claimed that their healing powers came from God. But those who cast curses (called "hexes") were generally felt to draw their power from a more demonic source.

The most prominent textbooks of hexerei were called "The Sixth and Seventh Books of Moses". In reality, these books were almost certainly completely fabricated by a man named Johann Scheibel, who lived in Stuttgart, Germany in the late 1700's. Readers at that time had a great fascination with the classical world and the occult. Unscrupulous authors profited from this by claiming to "discover" ancient magical texts, which they then "edited" and published.

The introduction to The Sixth and Seventh Books of Moses claims a much grander origin, of course. It states that these books were thousands of years old—revealed by God to Moses on Mount Sinai, passed down for generations until they were hidden by the High Priest Sadock in ancient Jerusalem. They were then recovered by the Roman Emperor Constantine and hidden in the Vatican by Pope Sylvester, who decreed that they never be made public "under pain of excommunication." By means of the charms revealed in this book, God supposedly gave Moses "might, power and wisdom to rule over the spirits of heaven and hell."

These books present a series of magical tables and seals by which various spirits could be summoned to do the conjurer's will. For example, the spirits of water can be summoned to "amply supply the treasures of the deep" by saying the following phrase: "I call upon and command thee Chananya by God Tetragrammaton Eloh. I conjure thee Yescaijah by Alpha and Omega, and thou art compelled through Adonai." (Don't worry, the author stresses that the charms only work if you say them in Hebrew.)

The "seals" in the book contain Hebrew characters and other writings that resemble Egyptian hieroglyphics. Many Latin words and phrases are mixed in for good measure, despite the fact that at the time the Sixth and Seventh Books of Moses claim to have been written, the Latin language probably didn't exist yet. (The city of Rome wasn't founded until almost 1000 years after God spoke to Moses on Mt. Sinai.)

Despite their historical inconsistencies, The Sixth and Seventh Books of Moses commanded a great deal of belief in Central Pennsylvania in the nineteenth and early twentieth centuries. Even owning a copy was felt to risk having one's soul damned to hell for all eternity. It was difficult to find someone who would admit actually casting a hex, but belief in hexes was powerful and any turn of bad luck was often blamed on them. People would spend a great deal of time and money trying to break the hold an imagined hex had on their lives.

Powwow doctors generated a lot of business by claiming to break hexes or protect their clients from future curses. John Hohman's "The Long Lost Friend" contains many prescriptions such as the following: "Like unto the cup and wine, and the holy supper, which our dear Lord Jesus Christ gave unto his disciples on Maundy Thursday, may the Lord Jesus guard me in daytime and at night, that…no witchcraft and enchantment can harm me. Amen."

If a braucher was not successful in breaking one's streak of bad luck, that just meant that the hex had been cast by a more powerful magician. Superstitious residents of Central Pennsylvania could spend years going from one powwow doctor to another, searching for one with the skill to break the curse. Some were known to spend thousands of dollars and many years on such a quest, without success. Desperate people could then be driven to commit drastic actions to try to free themselves and turn their lives around.

The most famous incident of this type was the case of John Blymire in 1928, and his confrontation with the witch of Rehmeyer's Hollow.

The Witch of Rehmeyer's Hollow

Many of the stories in this book resemble ghostly tales you might find in any city or county in the United States. But this one is different—it is pure York County. It could not have happened anywhere else.

The story starts with an unfortunate young man named John Blymire. He was thin and sickly, with a long birdlike nose and nervous eyes. His intelligence was at best felt to be "slow normal". But John Blymire had a special power. Both his father and grandfather were brauchers, or traditional Pennsylvania German folk healers. (See "Powwow", the previous story.)

Young John Blymire believed that the power of healing had been passed down to him as well. He began to have "visions" at the age of four, and at age seven he performed his first powwow cure, on his grandfather. The old man was suffering from urinary retention, probably the result of an enlarged prostate. The cure was a familiar combination of folk medicine and Christian prayer: Blymire's father killed a hog and removed its bladder, which John then burned to a crisp. He fed the ashes of the pig's bladder to his grandfather, then he made the sign of the cross and said the Lord's prayer three times. According to family reports, the old man's urinary retention vanished immediately, and never bothered him again.

As he grew up, Blymire continued to provide cures for his neighbors and a number of people around York. But his family was poor, and Blymire never earned enough money from his powwowing to make it a full time career. When he was ten years old he got a job digging potatoes for one of the most renowned brauchers in York County—Mr. Nelson Rehmeyer, referred to by locals as "the witch of Rehmeyer's Hollow".

Rehmeyer was a large, imposing man standing over six feet tall and weighing in excess of 200 pounds. He had dark eyes, and was said to be part German and part Susquehannock Indian. People drove or walked for miles to reach Rehmeyer's isolated farm in southern York County, seeking healing or other magical favors only a powerful powwow doctor could deliver. Although Blymire worked for him only for a few months, the witch of Rehmeyer's Hollow made quite an impression on him—one he would never forget.

Blymire left school at age 13 and held down a variety of odd jobs. He married in 1917, and for a while life seemed to be going pretty well for him. Then, a string of terrible luck began. Two of Blymire's three children died in infancy. He developed a continuous headache, and he lost a large amount of weight. He became extremely nervous, to the point where he would jump at even the slightest sound. Worst of all, from his point of view, his powwow magic ceased to work. He could no longer heal, and thus he lost the income and prestige that went along with being a braucher.

To Blymire, the reason for this bad luck was clear—some unknown enemy must have placed a hex on him. Hexes were the dark side of Pennsylvania folk magic. Hexes could cause their victim to suffer illness or financial ruin, sickness in cattle and trouble in relationships. Whenever a run of bad luck occurred to a York County family in the nineteenth and early twentieth centuries, it was common to suspect that some sort of hex had been cast upon them.

Powwow doctors derived a large part of their business from analyzing and counteracting these imagined hexes. Very few would admit to actually casting hexes on other people, since this was considered a form of dark magic. But belief in hexes was extremely strong—strong enough to drive some people to desperate measures in order to break them.

John Blymire began a quest to find the person who had cast the hex on him—a quest that would take more than ten years to reach its conclusion. He spent hundreds of dollars and countless hours consulting brauchers in York, Lancaster, and Lebanon counties, but to no avail. At one point he even suspected that his own wife was the culprit, and he began to accost her aggressively. She left him and married another man, saying she was afraid Blymire would kill her if she stayed with him. Blymire's depression and his desperation grew deeper.

Finally, in the summer of 1928, Blymire consulted Mrs. Nellie Noll, known as "the high priestess of Marietta" in western Lancaster County. Mrs. Noll was a tiny woman in her nineties who had been practicing powwow since her husband died on their honeymoon in 1854. After six visits, she told Blymire that she knew who had cast the hex on him—none other than his old employer, Nelson Rehmeyer. She also told Blymire that there were two ways he could break the curse. First, he could get a lock of Rehmeyer's hair and bury it six to eight feet underground. If this didn't work, he could acquire and destroy Rehmeyer's copy of the book "The Long Lost Friend", considered to be the bible of any powwow doctor. If he accomplished either of these tasks, the hex would be broken and Blymire would finally be a free man.

Along the way, Blymire had met up with two men who would help him. The first was John Curry, a fourteen year old orphan whose alcoholic stepfather would beat him terribly. The second was

Wilbert Hess, who was part of a farming family that had itself fallen on hard times. After a few more visits to the high priestess of Marietta, Blymire was able to convince Curry and Hess that they too were under the power of a hex cast by Nelson Rehmeyer. The three of them decided to work together against their common enemy. They would not give up until the hexes were finished.

Blymire's first move was to sit in his room alone meditating for ten days, in an attempt to master Rehmeyer by the force of his willpower alone. When this failed to produce any effect, he decided more direct action was necessary. On Monday, November 26, 1928 Blymire and John Curry made their way in the dead of night to Rehmeyer's house, and woke him up. However, Rehmeyer was even larger and more muscular than Blymire had remembered him. The two men talked for a while, but it soon became clear that Blymire would never be able to dominate Rehmeyer by psychological means alone, and if he wanted to dominate him physically he would need more help.

Blymire and Curry hitchhiked their way back to York the following day, and bought 25 feet of rope at a hardware store. That night, they enlisted Wilbert Hess to come with them to Rehmeyer's Hollow for the final showdown. They arrived at Rehmeyer's house close to midnight, with a full moon in the sky, and again pounded on the door until they woke him up. Blymire got right to the point—he demanded that Rehmeyer hand over his copy of "The Long Lost Friend". Rehmeyer only smiled, and taunted the younger men. His confidence in his own powers, both magical and physical, was absolute.

Blymire grew angry, and started the attack. He pushed a couch against Rehmeyer, and shouted for the other two to help him. The three of them were able to pin Rehmeyer to the floor. Blymire asked Curry to hand him some rope, but instead of tying it around Rehmeyer's hands or feet, he looped it around his neck and pulled it tight. Rehmeyer continued to kick and struggle.

Curry walked over to the wood pile and picked up a log. He swung the heavy piece of wood and struck Rehmeyer on the head once, then again. With the third blow he fractured Rehmeyer's skull, and blood poured across the floor. Rehmeyer gave a final groan, and lay still. Blymire stood up and cried "Thank God! The witch is dead!"

They continued to beat the body until it was almost beyond recognition. Then Curry picked up a lamp, poured the oil over Rehmeyer's corpse and set it aflame. The three men ran out of the house into the darkness, with the fire of the burning body growing brighter behind them. Blymire looked back once, and was seized with terror. He saw a huge black figure drift out of the house and start moving toward him. Was Rehmeyer still alive? Was it a ghost? Blymire was suddenly frozen in place. But then the black figure dissipated into smoke and was gone.

Rehmeyer's body was discovered several days later by a neighbor, who had heard the braying of an unfed mule in the barn. Blymire, Curry, and Hess were taken into custody less than twenty-four hours later. Their trial was an international sensation, as Rehmeyer's Hollow was mobbed by reporters from as far away as New York, London, and Paris. Cosmopolitan Americans could not believe that in the middle of the twentieth century witches were still killing each other in the farmlands of York County. Much was written about the "ignorant Dutchmen" of Pennsylvania, who still believed so strongly in hexes and powwow medicine.

The three men were convicted of murder, and over the years the sensationalism of the hex trials has faded away. But there are those who say that ghosts remain in Rehmeyer's Hollow. The partially burnt house in which Rehmeyer was murdered was rebuilt, and mysterious occurrences have been reported there over the years. Cars have stalled when driving past it, and dogs have started barking uncontrollably. Bloody handprints have been found on the walls, and fires have spontaneously begun and stopped there. It is said that if a Bible is placed on the foundation of the house, it will burst into flame.

In the area around the hollow, strange noises have been heard at night. One person reports meeting the ghost of Nelson Rehmeyer in a cornfield. The ghost tried to get the man to come closer, but when he refused the ghost vanished. Some say that the land itself is cursed there, and that it is difficult to grow crops. Could it be that Rehmeyer's hex was not broken by his murder—but was only made stronger? No one can say, but on the night of a full moon, when it's close to midnight, it's probably a good idea to steer your car away from Rehmeyer's Hollow.

Bibliography

This is a partial list of sources from print and the internet which I consulted in preparing this book. I also spoke to many individual people who have had ghostly experiences, most of whom did not wish to be mentioned by name. I am thankful to everyone who helped me, and I apologize for any I have left out.

1. "A History of Catholics in York, PA" by Abby Bowman.
http://ftp.rootsweb.com/pub/usgenweb/pa/york/church/cath-1927.txt
2. Accomac Inn – History.
http://www.accomacinn.com/history.shtm

3. "A Death Revisited" by Karen Muller. York Daily Record. June 14, 2003.

4. Camp Security. http://www.campsecurity.com

5. Camp Security: History. http://hometown.aol.com/stough1752/History.html

6. "City's Historic Ghosts: They're not where state put them" by Scott Miller. York Daily Record. June 1976.

7. Codorus Furnace by Scott D. Butcher, 2002. http://www.yorkliks.net/VirtYork/codorus.htm

8. Contemporary William Goodridge Articles. http://muweb.millersville.edu/-ugrr/yorkugrr/articles1.html

9. "Elmwood Mansion has its share" by David Gulden. York Sunday News. October 22, 2000.

10. Facts and Folklore of York PA by Georg R. Sheets. Osborn Printing Co. York, PA. 1993.

11. "Ghost Students of York PA". X Project: Paranormal Forum. http://p090.ezboard.com/fxprojectforumfrm8

12. Ghosttowns.com. http://forums.ghosttowns.com

13. Ghost Watch: Paranormal Investigation Agency. http://home.comcast.net/-ghostwatch

14. "Gravity Hill". Ghost Hunting in Pennsylvania. http://netlocity.net/ghost/investigations

15. "Haunted Places in PA Part 17". Butterfly Princess: mysterieschannel. www.mysterieschannel.com

16. Haunting with Wendall Woodberry, a video by Hellam Hills Productions and WJW Productions. CW Kondor Media. 1992.

17. "He Finds Peace in Haunted House" by Rita Beyer. The York Dispatch. October 31, 2001.

18. "Hesse Dhal" a poem by Henry L. Fisher. Translated from Pennsylvania Dutch by Paul and Katie Weisser.

19. "Hex Hollow and haunting tales" by Nerissa Miller. York Sunday News. October 22, 1995

20. Horrorfind Forums—Hex Hollow. http://www.horrorfind.com

21. "Idaho Ghosts" by Monica Grimm. http://idaho_ghosts.tripod.com

22. "James Smith: Signer of the Declaration of Independence". James Monroe.Org. http://www.rebelswithavision.com/James-Smith.net

23. "Legend says spooks haunt murder site" by Dave Gulden. York Sunday News. October 22, 2000.

24. Never to be Forgotten by James McClure. Strine Printing Company. York, PA. 1999.

25. Pennsylvania Dutch Country Ghosts, Legends and Lore by Charles Adams III. Exeter House Books. Reading PA. 1994.

26. "Philip Livingston" by Stefan Fielinkski. http://www.nysm.nysed.gov.albany/bios/I/phlivingston.html

27. "Pow-wow" by George Knowles. Controverscial.Com. http://www.controverscial.com/Pow-wow.htm

28. "Powwowing: A Persistent American Esoteric Tradition" by David W. Kriebel, Ph.D. http://www.esoteric.msu.edu/VolumeIV/Powwow.htm

29. "Re: 7 Gates of Hell". http://www.cosmicblessings.com

30. "Scare up some fun" by Barb Krebs. York Dispatch. October 11, 2002.

31. Shadowlands Haunted Places Index. http://theshadowlands.net

32. "Slaymaker's Ghost at Punkin Center" by H.C. Frey. York Heritage Trust Library.

33. The Battle of Trenton by Glenn Valis. August 4, 2003. http://www.doublegv.com/ggv/battles/Trenton.html

34. "The Haunted Cupboard" by Mary Kelly Mills. York Heritage Trust Library.

35. "The Helbenightians of Punkin Center" by H.C. Frey. York Heritage Trust Library.

36. "The Hex Story" by Georg R. Sheets. http://www.hexhollow.com

37. "The Spooks Again". York Daily Record. January 1880.

38. Urban Legends Research Center. http://www.ulrc.com.au/html/grimoire.asp

39. York Heritage Trust Archives

40. York Daily Record issues on October 31, 1980. October 29, 1999. October 26, 2000.

41. York Dispatch October 26, 2000.

42. York Sunday News October 22, 1995